Call Him By Name

A 25-Day Advent Devotional
Celebrating the Names of Jesus

Call Him By Name

A 25-Day Advent Devotional
Celebrating the Names of Jesus

Jeff Redmond

Kamel Press, LLC

Visit us at
www.KamelPress.com/Redmond

Copyright ©2023 by Jeff Luther Redmond. All rights reserved. Translation and/or reproduction are permissible upon request. Otherwise, no part of this book may be reproduced in any form or by any electronic or mechanical means without prior approval.

Unless otherwise noted, Scripture quotations are from the ESV® Bible (The Holy Bible, English Standard Version®), copyright© 2001 by Crossway Bibles, a publishing ministry of Good News Publishers. Used by permission. All rights reserved.

Proudly prepared for publication by Kamel Press, LLC
Cover design by Sherwin Muloc

ISBN-13:   978-1-62487-720-9 - Paperback
           978-1-62487-721-6 - eBook

Library of Congress Control Number: 2023949051

Published in the USA.

DEDICATION

To my wife, Kelley, who is always helping others in the Name of Jesus.

To my children and grandchildren, Jodie, Julie, Connor, Robert, and Abigail, who bring joy to Christmas beyond measure and are the first to remind me of Who Christmas is all about.

To my good friend, Keith, who is truly an inspiration and who read this devotional every Christmas ever since I gave him the first draft several years ago.

Contents

December 1 1
The Alpha and The Omega

December 2 4
Bright Morning Star

December 3 7
Christ, the Anointed One

December 4 11
The Door

December 5 14
Everlasting Father

December 6 17
Faithful and True

December 7 20
God Almighty

December 8 23
Horn of Salvation

December 9 26
Immanuel

December 10 29
Jesus, The Savior

December 11 33
King of Kings

December 12 35
The Lamb of God

December 13 38
Messiah

December 14	41
The Nazarene	

December 15 43
  Only Begotten Son, One and Only Son

December 16. 46
  Prince of Peace

December 17. 49
  Quencher of Our Thirst, Living Water

December 18. 53
  The Rock

December 19. 57
  Shepherd

December 20 60
  Truth

December 21 63
  Unmerited Favor, Grace

December 22 66
  The Vine, The Root, and The Branch

December 23 69
  The Word

December 24 73
  Xalted One, Exalted One

December 25 76
  Yahweh, I AM

  Zion's Precious Cornerstone

Afterword 79

December 1

THE ALPHA AND THE OMEGA
(Revelation 22:13)

What is unique about the following sentence?
"The quick brown fox jumps over the lazy dog." This sentence contains all twenty-six letters of the English alphabet. Put this under fun facts you may have already known (or hope to soon forget). May it also help you to remember the name of Jesus – **Alpha and Omega.**

Jesus said, *"I am the **Alpha and the Omega**, the First and the Last, the Beginning and the End"* (Revelation 22:13). The ***alpha and the omega*** being the first and last letters of the Greek alphabet; Jesus is the beginning of all things and the culmination of all that is to come. The apostle John tells us in John 1:2 that Jesus was in the beginning, before creation. He is eternal with no beginning or ending. Most people think of God the Father as the Creator God and while all three Persons of the Trinity are eternal and were involved in creation; however, the Bible clearly tells us Jesus made all things (John 1:3). The three Names of Revelation 22:13, (***Alpha and Omega***, *First and Last, Beginning and End*), are a reference to wholeness or completeness, meaning Jesus is fully God. We serve one God and we know Him as Father, Son, and Holy Spirit. The Son, Jesus, is fully God. There are twenty-two letters in the Greek alphabet and as Jesus is the Word, He uses all the letters of the alphabet in any language to express the truth about Jesus and His love for us.

When we were in preschool and kindergarten we learned about our ABCs. We sang songs that helped us to memorize the alphabet. We wrote words and drew pictures which began with each letter of the alphabet. When we memorized all the letters in order, we found somebody who cared enough to listen to let them know we knew our ABCs from A to Z. How much more important it is to learn all we can about Jesus. We need to sing songs at Christmas and throughout the year to help us to remember and celebrate. It is good when we write words and draw pictures and decorate to express our love for Him. But that's not all we need to do. We need to find others who will listen, to let them know we know our spiritual ABCs (All aBout Christ) and we have much more to learn about Jesus from A to Z (or from ***Alpha to Omega***).

Celebrating Jesus this Christmas

Here are some suggestions for the next twenty-five days (if you are reading this on December 1ˢᵗ):

- What are some ways you can get to know more and more about your Savior this Christmas?

  _____
  _____
  _____
  _____

- As you learn more about Christ's love, what are some ways you can express your love for Him?

  _____
  _____
  _____
  _____

- How can you show the kind of love you have learned from Him?

  _____
  _____
  _____
  _____

Pray: "***Alpha and Omega,*** send somebody my way in the next twenty-five days for whom I can share my testimony about You or share something I have learned about Your love. In Your Name, Amen."

December 2

BRIGHT MORNING STAR
(Revelation 22:16, 2 Peter 1:19)

In the last chapter of the Bible, immediately after Jesus called Himself the Alpha and the Omega, He calls Himself the ***Bright Morning Star***, *"I, Jesus, have sent My angel to testify to you about these things for the churches. I am the root and the descendant of David, the **Bright Morning Star**"* (Revelation 22:16). The morning star is the bright star that appears just before dawn. Sometimes it is the planet Venus that appears on the horizon just before the sun begins to shine to announce the coming of the new day. The morning star as it relates to Jesus is also mentioned in Revelation 2:28 and 2 Peter 1:19. After the long dark night, the ***Bright Morning Star*** is hope and encouragement of a new day. This name for Jesus certainly makes us think of the star that announced the coming of the Christ child 2000 years ago which was followed by the wise men of the east. One day Jesus is coming again. Jesus used this name for Himself so that we might have hope and assurance of His coming again. And today, even when things are at their darkest and times are tough, we can see Jesus, the ***Bright Morning Star,*** Who always gives hope and encouragement. Thank Jesus for the hope He gives you. You are not alone. His light wants to shine on you and through you to others.

Interestingly, the devil's proper name before the fall was Lucifer, which means, 'morning star'. But he is a deceiver and makes us think the night and the darkness will never end. If you look at or listen to the news or social media today, it is easy to get discouraged by the long list of bad news; which never seems to end. This Christmas if you look beyond the horizon and the present circumstances, you will see Jesus, the true ***Bright Morning Star***.

At the very beginning of the Covid-19 pandemic in the spring of 2020, members of our church were looking for a way to still reach out to

Celebrating Jesus this Christmas

people in our community, in particular to those in need. Just a few blocks from the church campus are government housing apartments, what we used to call "the projects". We had long talked about doing ministry for the people living there and even made some attempts in the past. The pandemic caused us to think of creative ways to minister. With a little organization and help from church members, but we began to deliver meals while wearing masks and gloves to each and every door that would open up to us. We probably should have sought permission first, but in these unprecedented times, we thought forgiveness would have been easier. A small group willing to venture out (while most people were hunkered down) began knocking on doors. The meals were well received by almost every home. After the first attempt, we delivered meals every week for the first few months. It was not long before we started asking for prayer needs. Since that time, we have delivered thousands of meals and prayed hundreds of prayers. We have monthly projects such as block parties and day camps. We have made many friends, shared the gospel multiple times, and, as of this writing, two men have prayed to receive Jesus as their personal Savior. We now have permission from the local authorities.

Even in the darkest of times, Jesus is not just the silver lining, He continues to be the ***Bright Morning Star*** Who gives hope for the future... and for today.

Call Him by Name

*"We also have the prophetic word strongly confirmed, and you will do well to pay attention to it, as to a lamp shining in a dark place, until the day dawns and **The Morning Star** rises in your hearts"* (2 Peter 1:19, CSB).

- ➢ What are the times or reasons during the Christmas season, or soon thereafter, that might cause you to feel down or depressed?

_____
_____
_____
_____

- ➢ Write down a verse or its reference for you to memorize to remind you of the hope and encouragement found in Jesus for the duration of this Christmas season and beyond:

_____
_____
_____
_____

- ➢ What part of the Christmas story, for you, helps you to remember Jesus cares and understands like no other?

_____
_____
_____
_____

Pray: "***Bright Morning Star***, help me to remember my emotions and feelings may run high and low this time of year, but Your love and care for me is steadfast. I will put my faith in You. In Your Name, Amen."

December 3

CHRIST, THE ANOINTED ONE
(John 7:40-43)

Don't take **Christ** out of Christmas! You have probably heard it before or maybe you have seen 'Merry Xmas' written somewhere and thought it sure seems sacrilegious. Actually, the Greek capital letter Chi which looks like a capital X was an early Christian symbol for **Christ**. But when written, the X would drop halfway below the line. So next time you see 'Merry Xmas', look to see if the X has dropped below the line a little, otherwise you are probably right and you want to remember not to leave **Christ** out of Christmas. (or say, "Great, I didn't know you knew Greek!")

In the New Testament, the name of **Christ** is written along with the name, Jesus, 195 times in 185 verses. In learning some of the basics of Bible study, we understand that repetition and space are to be considered. In other words, if something is repeated often, it must be important. **Christ** means, *'The Anointed One'*. It is not just a name, it is a title. Even some who did not believe in Jesus while He was on the earth, were looking for The **Christ** – the long-awaited Messiah. Read the argument of some of the Jewish people who listened to Jesus,

> *"When they heard these words, some of the people said, 'This really is the Prophet.' Others said, 'This is the **Christ**.' But some said, 'Is the **Christ** to come from Galilee? Has not the Scripture said that the **Christ** comes from the offspring of David, and comes from Bethlehem, the village where David was?' So there was a division among the people over Him." (John 7:40-43)*

Call Him by Name

    Isn't it interesting that without knowing it, they pointed to the fact that Jesus was from the line of David and born in Bethlehem? Thus, this name and title for Jesus reminds us He fulfilled every prophecy of the Old Testament. He was actually physically anointed twice, once by Mary, the sister of Martha and Lazarus, and once by an unknown woman in the home of Simon the Pharisee. In the Old Testament, two offices were anointed, that of kings and priests. As the King, Jesus holds ultimate rule and authority. As the High Priest, Jesus offered the greatest and last needed sacrifice for our sins and intercedes on our behalf.

Celebrating Jesus this Christmas

The Jewish people longed for their *Christ* Who would be their Deliverer, but most missed Him and refused to believe because they were looking for a political deliverer, or their religion and ritual were their only focus.

> Have you placed your faith in the one and only Jesus *Christ* for salvation?

_____

_____

_____

_____

If not, read Romans 10:9-13, and put your life and eternal life in His hands.

> If you know Jesus *Christ* and have trusted Him for eternal salvation, then list some specific areas you need to give over to Him today:

_____

_____

_____

_____

_____

Please do not miss how He wants to be your *Christ* every day and deliver you from your worry, anxiety, and non-purposeful existence on earth.

Today, Pray to receive *Christ* as your Savior (see next page). If you know Jesus as Savior, pray not to leave *Christ* out of Christmas or out of any day of your life.

<u>A Simple Prayer for Salvation</u>

Dear God,

I am a sinner who is in need.

Today, I turn from my sins and turn to You.

I believe Jesus Christ is Your Son.

I believe Jesus Christ died for my sins and rose again.

Forgive me of all my sins.

I want Jesus Christ to come into my heart and take control of my life.

I trust Jesus Christ as my Savior and will follow Him as my Lord.

In the name of Jesus Christ, I pray. Amen.

December 4

THE DOOR
(John 10:9)

Jesus used this name in John 10 to describe Himself as the Good Shepherd and we are His sheep. He said, *"I am **The Door**. If anyone enters by Me, he will be saved and will go in and out and find pasture"* (John 10:9).

When we think of a door – we think of a door like we used to get into our house. But in this case, it was simply an opening. And when we read that Jesus is **The Door**, we often hear or use that phrase to talk about Jesus being the way to salvation. Hear me close – Jesus *is* the way to salvation and He is the only way. John 10:9 (NIV), *"I am the gate; whoever enters through Me will be saved."* But the crux of Jesus being ***The Door*** is an understanding of those who are already His sheep on the inside of the door.

The opening of the sheep pen had no swinging door or gate, it was simply an opening, and often the shepherd would become ***the door*** and would spend the night laying down in the opening known as the gate watching over and protecting the sheep from thieves and robbers and those who would steal or harm the sheep. How appropriate as we think about the shepherds who first heard the news about the birth of Jesus.

This is the picture of Jesus: If you are on the outside there is only one way in. And when you enter, it is because you are invited by Jesus, and by His grace through faith you are saved. But once you are in, for those of us who are already in, we are not only saved, we also have a home and a place in this world and direction for today and every day.

I share this story for illustration purposes only: A few years ago, I had to have some oral surgery taken care of by a dentist who specializes in this kind of thing. (I'll spare you the details as to why…) He said, "We can do this one of two ways. I can put you to sleep with gas and you will not know anything that is going on and when you wake up, it will all be over. But the gas is a little more expensive. Or you can drink this 'I don't care juice' and you will be awake, but you really won't care and will not remember, but afterward you will *not* need to drive and you will need to go home and take it easy the rest of the day."

I said, "Listen Doc, the gas seems kind of expensive, but I also have a lot to do today. You are going to numb me up anyway right? Couldn't you just do the surgery and I don't take the gas, and I don't drink 'the juice'? Is that a possibility?" He said, "Yes, we could do that, but *I don't recommend it*." After some further discussion, I said, "Let's go for it."

He turned me upside down in the chair and without any kind of anesthesia, only a numbing of the gums, he yanked, pulled, drilled, and cut. I believe it was the most miserable hour I have ever spent. I think he was getting me back for not taking his advice. Afterward, I felt I had been hit by a Mack truck and gone the distance with Rocky Balboa and Apollo Creed at the same time. Next time a doctor or a dentist says, *"I wouldn't recommend it,"* I'm going to listen.

Can I tell you today that you can celebrate Christmas this year, live your life and go through crises and situations, and even face death and the afterlife - living without Jesus, living outside ***The Door*** instead of inside.... but *I would not recommend it*!

Celebrating Jesus this Christmas

Thank Jesus today, Who is ***The Door***, and look to Him for protection and direction.

> What might be the biggest crises you have faced this year?

_____
_____
_____
_____

> In what ways have you seen God protect you or help you through your crises?

_____
_____
_____
_____

> What might be the most difficult part of Christmas for you this year?

_____
_____
_____
_____

Pray: "Thank You Jesus. Help me to see You are ***The Door*** of the sheepfold, watching over and protecting me. Even my greatest crises cannot bring me harm, for You are always at work for good to those who know and love You and are called by Your great Name. Amen."

December 5

EVERLASTING FATHER
(Isaiah 9:6)

That's right, according to Isaiah 9:6, Jesus, the Son of God, is called ***Everlasting Father.*** The fifth name for Jesus may lead us to some difficulty in understanding if we think about it too long. We know God as The Trinity, the Three in One. He is the Father, Son, and the Holy Spirit. Yet Isaiah calls Jesus, Everlasting Father. Do you see the problem some might have with this title or name for the One we call God the Son?

The solution? Let's not think about it too much so as to not have too much difficulty with it... not really. Never be afraid to have questions and to search God's Word for answers. While questions and criticisms come and go, God's Word stands forever. It might help us to understand that the title 'father' in the Old Testament was used in many ways. It was often used out of respect for persons in authority like governors, priests, and prophets. While the Old Testament demanded respect for a Holy God, the coming of the Christ child represents that same respect, with the possibility of a new relationship with the eternal.

Jesus presented an aspect of God almost completely unknown to most of the world. For it is only in Jesus that we can know God as Father. Our best would be to combine the respect of the Old Testament and the personal relationship of the New Testament in our view of God. We are able to do this in the Person of Jesus Christ our Savior.

But maybe our focus should not be just on Jesus as Father, but on the everlasting eternal aspect of our Savior. Jesus did not start to exist in Bethlehem. He has always existed. He has no beginning or ending. Hebrews 13:8 says, *"Jesus Christ is the same yesterday and today and forever."* Thus, maybe the hard question is not, why would we call Jesus

Celebrating Jesus this Christmas

Father? The harder question might be to understand why would Jesus, the Eternal One, leave a perfect heaven to come to a very imperfect earth?

While you think about that... It is at Christmas time you see a lot of relatives and family. Some are a little more 'different' than others. I have an uncle who loves hummingbirds. He feeds them and reads about them. He said that hummingbirds do not flock like other birds. They are loners. In the spring, they will make their way north. The male will come first followed by the female at a later date. They will have little hummingbirds. Then in the fall, it is the female that is the first to go to the south. They will often make their way over Florida and miles of ocean before turning to South America and a warmer climate. After that, the male will follow, leaving the small baby hummingbird behind. At certain times of the year, you will only see the very small baby hummingbird around. But after a few days, the baby hummingbird will fly south and go all alone right where he is supposed to be. How? It is instinct. It's God's design and order. (How cool is that?)

When it comes to how much God cares for us, Jesus told us to look up and to look at what? *The birds of the air*... And we are so much more important to Him! Okay, the answer is hard to believe, but simple. Jesus is called Everlasting Father because JTAGS, (Jesus The Almighty God and Savior) cares for you!

Call Him by Name

Lift His name up in praise today because He is worthy of respect, and thank Him for His loving care. If you see a bird flying south today, remember the words of Jesus.

> What is one way today you can show respect to Jesus, Who is the ***Everlasting Father?***

_____
_____
_____
_____
_____
_____

> Name at least two ways Jesus has proven His desire to have a personal relationship with you.

_____
_____
_____
_____
_____
_____

Pray: "Dear Jesus, ***The Everlasting Father***, hallowed be Thy Name. I come before You with awe and reverence. Who am I that You would make Your way to know me? May I live a life worthy of Your call on my life. In Your Name, Amen."

December 6

Faithful and True
(*Revelation 19:11*)

John wrote in Revelation 19:11 (NKJV), *"Now I saw heaven opened, and behold, a white horse. And He who sat on him was called **Faithful and True...**"* Can we have a more appropriate name(s) for Jesus? He is always faithful and can always be trusted. Every Word He says is true and can be relied upon. In fact, it is not just true. It becomes truth because He says it. The White Horse Jesus comes riding on will be the final victory in the second coming. Do you believe it to be true that He is coming again? Sure you do. Do you really believe that Jesus was born of a virgin in Bethlehem to be the Savior of the world? I have no doubt that it is true. If we believe in the past, that Jesus was born in Bethlehem and is the Savior of the world, and if we believe in the future that Jesus, ***Faithful and True***, is coming again riding on a white horse, then why do we have such a hard time trusting Jesus to be ***Faithful and True*** in our everyday life and in difficult times?

I have heard the following illustration in various forms. I thought it might be appropriate for today: Twin boys, who looked just alike, but were so very different. One of the boys was always polite and compliant and appreciative of everything their mom and dad did for them. The other twin, not so much. He was always complaining, never helped out around the house, or showed appreciation for all his parents' love. Christmas was approaching. Mom and dad asked the boys to make out their Christmas list. You can guess which boy had the longer list. On Christmas morning, the ungrateful twin dove into the presents and opened everything under the tree that had his name on it, not showing any appreciation or barely pausing to grab the next gift, until all his gifts were opened, and, though he got everything on his list, he remained less than satisfied.

The other twin waited patiently until his brother was finished opening all the gifts. Even though he realized there were no gifts left under the tree for him. His parents said, "We are sorry, son, we did not get you anything on your list. But we do have something for you in the barn." They walked outside to the barn. His brother complained that he had to go outside. When they opened the barn door, there was a pile of manure waiting for him. The grateful twin actually dove into the pile of manure and started jumping with glee. Even his parents were surprised at his reaction and asked why he was so happy. He said, "Because I know if there is manure, somewhere there must be a pony!"

Next time life delivers you the hard, the difficult, or the less-than-pleasing circumstance - you can jump with glee, because somewhere in the not-so-distant future – there is a pony!

> *"Then I saw heaven opened, and behold, a white horse! The one sitting on it is called **Faithful and True**, and in righteousness He judges and makes war. His eyes are like a flame of fire, and on His head are many diadems, and He has a name written that no one knows but Himself. He is clothed in a robe dipped in blood, and the name by which He is called is The Word of God" (Revelation 19:11-13, ESV).*

Celebrating Jesus this Christmas

> How is it possible to *rejoice at all times*, as the Bible says?

_____
_____
_____
_____
_____
_____
_____
_____

> Yesterday, you named some difficulties you have faced or will face in the future. Can you write down at least one way Jesus, Who is ***Faithful and True,*** can use your difficulty for your good or someone else's?

_____
_____
_____
_____
_____
_____
_____
_____

Pray: "To The One Who is ***Faithful and True***, help me to increase my faith, especially in the most difficult and hard-to-understand situations. Lord, I believe. Help my unbelief! In Your Name, Amen."

December 7

GOD ALMIGHTY
(Isaiah 9:6, Luke 1:49)

Jesus is first called the ***Almighty God*** by the prophet Isaiah in his prophecy about the coming Child to be born. *"For unto us a Child is born, unto us a Son is given; And the government will be upon His shoulder. And His name will be called Wonderful, Counselor, **Mighty God**, Everlasting Father, Prince of Peace"* (Isaiah 9:6, NKJV). It is actually the name El-Gibbor, meaning ***God Almighty.*** Many times, already we have seen and claimed that Jesus is God, and as God, He is all-powerful.

This month you will hear many other names for Jesus, but I also want you to use the next few days to look for evidence of God's power revealed in your life and in those around you. He is powerful enough to raise the dead, make the lame to walk, open the eyes of the blind, and feed the multitude. Do not believe that His power is limited today. Maybe you have known of this kind of miraculous power in your life or in the life of someone close to you. If so, give praise to Jesus Who is ***God Almighty***. Even if you have never seen what you think is a true physical miracle, it does not mean His power is limited. No, Indeed! For sometimes God's power is revealed when there is hope that comes out of tragedy.

A lot of negative things happen in life that we cannot fully explain or understand; things like illness, mass shootings, and other personal crises. People might ask, "If there is a God and He is all-powerful, why do these things happen?" I wish I could explain it adequately and fully, but I can't. We do live in a sinful fallen world due to our sins and the sins of others. We are witnessing the consequences of sin.

I also know the Lord is powerful enough to do as He pleases and stop bad things from happening. I believe He does prevent tragedies more than we know. When He does not, we must still trust Him. Perhaps it is an even greater power revealed when He works in the midst

Celebrating Jesus this Christmas

of tough situations and works in us and through us to show His great mercy and grace so that lives are changed and people are brought to Jesus. Forgiveness, obedience, and love shown in and through you are powerful tools in the hands of Jesus. These are also evidence of God's power at work in a believer's life. The greatest power of all is still in a transformed life which was once lost and now is saved by the miraculous work of Jesus, Whom we now know as ***God Almighty***.

Watch this week for evidence of God's power in your life and the life of others. Proclaim today the praise that Mary did in Luke 1 after hearing of The Child to be born to her. Mary proclaimed, *"For He **Who is Mighty** has done great things for me, and holy is His name"* (Luke 1:49). While it is not a Christmas song, consider claiming the lyrics of contemporary Christian singer David Crowder this year as you celebrate Jesus, "*Good **God Almighty**, I hope You'll find me praising Your Name no matter what comes.*"

➢ Today, begin to list evidences of God's power in your life and those around you:

_____
_____
_____
_____
_____

➢ If you truly believed God was all-powerful, what would you ask God to do?

_____
_____
_____
_____
_____

Pray: "***God Almighty***, thank You for powerfully transforming my life to make me a member of Your holy family. Draw me close to You so that I might be able to experience more of Your wonderful mighty work in my life and see more of Your kingdom-building work. I give You praise. For You, ***God Almighty,*** have done great things for me. In Your Name, Amen."

December 8

HORN OF SALVATION
(Luke 1:69)

"And (He) *has raised up a **Horn of Salvation** for us in the house of His servant David"* (Luke 1:69). Okay, if you were looking for a new name for Jesus, this may be it. Up until now the first week of names have been fairly familiar. This name, or title, was given by Zachariah, the Father of John the Baptist, on the day John was born. John's birth represented the preparation of the coming Savior. John, the second cousin of Jesus, would preach repentance to prepare the people for Jesus' message of hope and salvation. You might remember that Zachariah was a priest to whom an angel spoke and told that he and his wife, who had no children and were now senior adults, would have a child who would preach about the good news of the Lord's coming. For another Child would be born Who would be the Savior of the World.

Zachariah doubted. I tend to think as a priest chosen by God, he doubted about the 'birth thing' and not about God's power to redeem. For those of us who have been on this earth for 60 or more years, we can relate. He at least sought to be gracious toward his wife. He said, *"I am an old man,* (and gee), *my wife is advanced in years"* (Luke 1:18). That was a nice way of saying that she is old, too. Nevertheless, the angel Gabriel struck him dumb for doubting. He could not speak until John was born. (By the way, I am stopping myself from telling a joke about God's grace; trading the ability to talk versus the ability to reproduce… feel free to insert your own).

Call Him by Name

When John was born, they asked him the name of the baby. As soon as Zechariah wrote the name John, *"his mouth was opened and his tongue was loosed"*. He praised and prophesied about the coming Messiah, and one of the first things out of Zechariah's mouth was this name for Jesus, the ***Horn of Salvation***. It was a name used in the Old Testament to represent the strength of God. In Deuteronomy 33, Moses wrote that the tribes of Israel, with God leading them into the Promised Land, would be like the horns of a wild ox as they pushed the people out of the land. David wrote in Psalm 18 after being delivered from the hand of his enemies, *"The LORD is my rock and my fortress and my deliverer, my God, my rock, in whom I take refuge, my shield, and the **horn of my salvation**, my stronghold."* The ***Horn of Salvation*** is used among a plethora of names and descriptions praising the strength of the Lord.

He has the power to give eternal salvation and the strength to sustain us in our everyday walk with Him. Have you ever doubted God? Ever have doubts about your salvation, or if God was really going to come through for you or make Himself known? If you have had doubts, you are in good company, most of us have. If you say you have never had doubts, you might have a bigger problem. (It's called lying.) Yes, I have heard preachers say, "If you have doubts, you must not be saved." But I don't find that to be very biblical. However, doubts do not usually come when we are at our best. Doubts usually come when we are weak. But for most of us, we have doubts from time to time. Doubting is not a sin. It is what you do with your doubts that is important. Take them to Jesus, and ask for His reassurance. Doubting *can* lead to sin, so be careful. But it *can* also help you to grow even more confident when you confess your doubts to God. I will let you in on a secret. He knows anyway. And here is good news...Where we are weak, He is strong. Thus, the name – ***Horn of Salvation!***

Celebrating Jesus this Christmas

> I am giving you permission to list any doubts you have today, or have had in the recent past:

_____
_____
_____
_____
_____
_____

> Write at least one thing Jesus said or did that should give you reassurance:

(Hint: If you can't think of anything, something about Christmas or Easter will suffice.)

_____
_____
_____
_____
_____
_____

Pray: "Dear Jesus, ***Horn of Salvation***, please take any doubts I have and remind me of Your promises. Take my moments of weakness and give me strength as I learn to trust less in myself and more in You. In Your Name, Amen."

December 9

IMMANUEL
(Isaiah 7:14, Matthew 1:23, Matthew 28:20)

No list of names of Jesus at Christmas time would be complete without the name ***Immanuel***. The question I get asked most about this name is, "Do you spell that name with an 'I' or with an 'E'?" The answer is *yes*. Since it is a phonetic transliteration of the Hebrew, either would be correct. But as you can see, I spell it with an I. You have every right to be a little wrong and not spell it the way I do. (Have I impressed you yet with the term 'phonetic transliteration'? I didn't think so. It just means that is how the name sounds in the original language.)

We have five names for Jesus in Isaiah 9. But before those names were given, Immanuel was the name given to Jesus in Isaiah 7, *"Therefore the Lord Himself will give you a sign. Behold, the virgin shall conceive and bear a son, and shall call His name **Immanuel**"* (Isaiah 7:14). Actually, there has been a long debate among scholars and people who care about such things about whom this prophecy was about. And there has been some controversy over the Hebrew word for virgin, which can also be translated as young unmarried woman. That is, until Matthew wrote his gospel in the New Testament. This is the very first Old Testament quote and fulfillment in the New Testament. Matthew writes that an angel from heaven appeared to Joseph, the fiancé to pregnant Mary, and he foretells the birth of Jesus and the angel quotes this verse in Isaiah. Matthew leaves no doubt, that the prophet was talking about Jesus. And the word used in the Greek language for Mary can only mean virgin and nothing else. But that's not all. For those of us who might not be familiar with the name ***Immanuel***, Matthew, the disciple of Jesus and gospel writer, adds a parenthetical note that was not part of the original prophecy in Isaiah. At the end of the verse in Matthew 1:23, he writes, - *"this name of Jesus means, God with us."* Matthew was so clear in making sure we, who read the Bible, or at least the Christmas story parts, are sure to understand what Matthew wanted us to know about Jesus. Matthew left no doubt about the one called ***Immanuel***, He was God Who dwelt among us.

I wonder if people who read our lives, watch our actions, or hear our words are clear about what we say we believe about Jesus. During this Christmas season, when it comes to what you believe - if you have experienced the transformational love of Jesus, and if He dwells with you – leave no doubt!

That really should be enough for one day and one name. And if you want to stop reading right here, it is completely understandable, ... (pausing long enough for you to stop reading). This name and prophecy are so rich in meaning. I recall sometime back watching Late Night with David Letterman, and he was interviewing Larry King (I know, old school names. What can I say?). David Letterman asked Larry King, "If you could interview anyone, living or dead, who would it be?" Without hesitation, Larry King, who is Jewish, said, "I would want to interview Jesus Christ." Lettermen said, "What would you ask Jesus?" King's response, "Were you really born of a virgin?" There was a pregnant pause (some pun intended) as if Lettermen did not know what to say next. Lettermen looked at the camera and said, "We will be right back after these commercial messages."

Yes, it does make all the difference. The only way Jesus could be Immanuel, God with us, is if He was born of a virgin and the unique heaven-born Son of God. He is God incarnate, God in the flesh, Who dwelt among us and still does today. He took the initiative to make His way to us who did not deserve His presence nor His love, but He came anyway.

Call Him by Name

Matthew started and ended his gospel assuring us of the presence of Jesus Who never leaves us. *"And lo, I am with you always, even to the end of the age. Amen"* (Matthew 28:20b, NKJV).

> Can you identify any words or actions that would make it unclear to others you belong to Jesus or you really believe in Him?

_____
_____
_____
_____
_____
_____

> What can you change or do to leave no doubt you believe Jesus is God in the flesh and you belong to Him?

_____
_____
_____
_____
_____

Pray: "Dear ***Immanuel,*** I cannot mention Your name without praise and thanksgiving for coming in the flesh and dwelling among us. Your presence and promise make every day worth living. As I live in the flesh, may others be able to see You living in me. May my words and actions leave no doubt I believe in You. In Your Name, Amen."

December 10

JESUS, THE SAVIOR
(Matthew 1:21, Luke 1:32)

Now, for the most familiar name for our Lord and its meaning and significance: Both Mary and Joseph were told to name the baby *Jesus*. The name means Savior or 'Jehovah is Salvation'. It is the Greek transliteration (there is that word again!) of the Hebrew name for Joshua. It was a common name among the Jewish people, and though not uncommon today, most parents are slow to name a child *Jesus* today (a little more common among the Latino world). No Jewish person in Jesus' day would have heard His name and not thought of Joshua, the great conqueror of the Old Testament, and its meaning. Yet, most missed recognizing *Jesus as Savior,* or refused to believe. Consider this year there are still many parts of the world where Christmas comes and goes without notice because they have yet to hear the name of *Jesus*. We are on a quest to tell more and more people about *Jesus, The Savior* of the world.

However, in our culture in the United States, it would be hard to believe people have not at least heard the name of *Jesus* and that we celebrate His birth on December 25th. It does not matter how many schools have traded the name Christmas break for the Winter holiday or how many nativity scenes are taken off city, state, and federal lawns, most people know why there are traffic jams and crowded shopping centers in December. It does not matter if people put Xmas instead of Christmas (okay it matters to me), or if they will only say Happy Holidays (feel free to respond with a 'Merry Christmas,' although you cannot say holiday without the word holy... but that's for another day), people know we are celebrating *Jesus*' birthday. I know not every American celebrates Christmas. However, many have never stepped foot in a church, never read the Bible, and don't really know *Jesus* - who celebrate His birthday. By the way, this week or next when you are stuck in slow traffic, instead of experiencing a little driver's rage, pause long enough to reflect how amazing it is that a little baby born in the small town of Bethlehem can cause a traffic jam over 2000 years removed and 7000 miles away... I'm just saying!

But here is my question. How can so many people hear the name of Jesus at Christmas time, every year in our country and so many other places around the world and most remain virtually unchanged? Perhaps the answer is found in Scripture (as it always is). When the angel told Joseph to name the baby *Jesus*, he added, *"Because He will save His people from their sins"* (Matthew 1:21, NIV).

A few years ago, my wife Kelley and I took a trip out west which included a visit to the Grand Canyon. We stayed for a couple of days. One of the things we noticed was how friendly were the deer in the park of the canyon. They were not skittish about tourists. They would walk right up to you, seemingly wanting something to eat. But there were signs and the park rangers told us not to feed the deer, as it would be unhealthy. We heeded the warning. It was not long after our trip that I just happened to hear that park rangers had to go to the bottom of the canyon and kill thirty or more of the deer who were dying of starvation. There was plenty of food and natural vegetation for the deer to eat, but the deer had eaten so much of the bad food from tourists and eaten the garbage left behind, so now they could no longer digest the good food they needed to survive.

The celebration of the birth of Jesus is a wonderful and blessed thing we do. I do believe and have known many who have been transformed by Jesus at Christmas time because they have heard the good news. But for so many, they cannot digest the eternal things of God, because they have picked up and taken in the garbage of this world. The name of Jesus and the good news is all around, but until something is done about sin in our life, we cannot take in the truth and experience the transforming power of *Jesus*. *Jesus* said, *"Unless you repent, you will all likewise perish"* (Luke 13:3). Even for genuine believers, we pick up the trash of this world so easily and are still sinners saved by grace, but unless we confess our sins to *Jesus* daily, we will miss out on the spiritual nourishment the Lord has for us, so we might grow and mature.

There is another clue for us in the Christmas story of why people are still missing *Jesus*. The angel told Mary right after he told her to call Him *Jesus*, *"He will be great and will be called Son of the Most High"* (Luke 1:32). Could it be that people are believing in the wrong Jesus? He is not the cuss word or the butt of a joke. He is more than the warm fuzzy feeling we might get on Christmas morning. He is not anything less than the true and only God Who came to be the Savior of the world. I am asked from time to time, "Are Mormons and Jehovah's Witnesses going to heaven? Are they Christians?" Not if they believe in the doctrine and theology of their church. It is true they have some strange teachings (as many think Baptists do). But here is where it really matters... It is what they teach about *Jesus*. They may use some of the same phrases like Son of God, but if you search, you will discover their Jesus is less than the biblical *Jesus*. He is portrayed as something less. This is not about putting down other religions or cults. We want all people to believe in the real biblical *Jesus* - born in Bethlehem, died on Calvary, and rose again.

Sometime back I began to use the acronym JTAGS, which stands for '***Jesus The Almighty God and Savior***'. It entails more than one name we have used so far. I have used it personally and in sermons and at times when talking in code with missionaries living in closed countries. Just like an 'ichthus' means fish for fishers of men. (The Greek acronym *ichthus* stands for Jesus Christ God's Son & Savior.) JTAGS means we are tagged by Jesus, and we belong to Him. I don't know if it will catch on with others, but it is one way I am identified with the real Jesus. And it is a great conversation starter.

Call Him by Name

What do you need to do today? Confess, repent, and believe in the real Jesus. Then, and only then, can celebrating the birth of Jesus transform your life and others.

➢ Identify any sins you have yet to confess. Write them down, if you dare:

_____
_____
_____
_____
_____
_____
_____
_____
_____

Pray: "Dear ***Jesus, the Savior*** of the world and my Savior, I confess my sins to You today. The closer the calendar gets to Christmas Day, may I draw even closer to You. Help me not to miss You and where You are at work in my life. May I also help others not to miss celebrating You this Christmas. In Your Name, Amen."

December 11

KING OF KINGS
(Revelation 19:16)

Does Jesus have a tattoo? Do you know why I ask? In the book of Revelation, John wrote about Jesus' second coming and this is what he saw, *"On His robe and on His thigh He has a name written,* ***King of Kings*** *and Lord of Lords."* Whenever someone asks me if it is a sin to have a tattoo, I direct them to Revelation 19:16. All the while I realize Jesus has a heavenly body and Revelation is full of symbols. Nevertheless, it is all true! Have you noticed the book of Revelation has some great names for Jesus? Always read Revelation for what it teaches us about Jesus and not just for symbols and apocalyptic events. Among the names in Revelation, ***King of Kings*** is prominent. Jesus is of the line and lineage of King David, and *"of His kingdom there will be no end"* (2 Samuel 7:16).

The Magi followed the star to Bethlehem. King Herod felt threatened because a new King had been born. Pilate placed a sign above the cross of Christ that read "This is the King of the Jews." When the Jewish leaders complained and asked Pilate to put, "He claimed to be King of the Jews", Pilate said, *"el graphe, el graphe"* – *"What I have written, I have written"* (John 19:22). Without realizing it, Pilate declared Him King! He has always been ***King of Kings***. He left the throne room to come to earth. He was King in the manger and on the cross. And when He comes again. He is worthy of honor and all glory. Contrary to most kings, He came to serve His people. The kings of Israel were supposed to be that kind of servant king. David came the closest. Jesus perfected it.

But it gets better. The New Testament teaches that those of us who are born into the family of God are of a *"royal priesthood"* (1 Peter 2:9). We are part of a kingly family with access to all the riches of The kingdom-riches that are not of this world. Most of us have barely tapped into the riches of The Kingdom which include things like peace, hope, love, and more than we could hope for or imagine. With privileges come responsibility. We serve The Kingdom and use the riches He has given us to help and influence others. Jesus is still the servant *King* and He uses His family, people like you and me, to do His important work.

> Take a moment and reflect on the majesty of the *King of Kings*. What images come to mind?

_____

_____

_____

_____

_____

> You might want to read Psalms 8, 18, or 28. Write down one or more significant attributes the Psalmist sees in the majesty of *The King of Kings*:

_____

_____

_____

_____

_____

Pray: "*King of Kings*, it is with awe and wonder I come before You today to consider Your majesty and splendor. Praise Your magnificent Name. Help me to be more submissive to Your perfect will. Help me to follow Your example of serving others. In Your Name, Amen."

(Yes, this one is shorter than the last couple of days. It is okay to go back and read now what you only glanced at before.)

December 12

THE LAMB OF GOD
(Isaiah 53:7, Revelation 5:6, John 1:29)

We don't bring sheep to church anymore! You can thank Jesus for that. But if there is one animal that seems to be dominant in the Scriptures. It is *The Lamb*. Technically a lamb is a young sheep. Back in Genesis, when Abraham was tested and asked to take his only son, Isaac, to be sacrificed. Isaac looked up at his dad and asked, "Where is *the lamb*...?" (Hang on to that question). In Exodus, when the Israelites had been in bondage for 400 years, God sent an angel of death as the tenth plague to kill all of the firstborn of Egypt. The Israelites were to sacrifice a lamb and put the blood on the doorposts as symbols of God's salvation. The Passover celebration is a remembrance of that night as lambs are used as a sacrifice and part of the meal. Leviticus teaches God's people about how they are to give sacrifices using *the lamb*. Isaiah gave the prophecy of a Messiah, *"He was led like a **lamb** to the slaughter, and as a sheep before its shearers is silent, so He did not open His mouth."* Every *lamb* in the Old Testament and every sacrifice pointed to Jesus. The sacrifices did not take away their sins, nor did they bring salvation. People were saved in the Old Testament the same way they are saved in the New Testament – *"By grace through faith."* When we are saved, we look back to what Jesus has done for us. They looked forward to a coming Messiah – the *Lamb of God*, the final sacrifice.

The *Lamb of God* is dominant in the New Testament. Twenty-eight times in the book of Revelation Jesus is referred to as *The Lamb*. One of my favorite chapters in Revelation is chapter 5, *"Then I saw a **Lamb**, looking as if it had been slain, standing..."* (verse 6). There is Jesus. He is the perfect *Lamb* (lambs that were sacrificed in the Old Testament had to be unblemished). He has been sacrificed for my sins and for your sins. He is the final and ultimate sacrifice. And He is standing. He is alive and continues to intercede on your behalf.

I guess it is somewhat ironic that Jesus, the ***Lamb of God***, was put into a feeding trough when He was born. Matthew and Luke supply us with many of the details of His birth. Then we are left with little detail about Jesus' growing up years, except His visit to the temple when He was twelve. But at the age of thirty, Jesus suddenly appears on the scene, and the very first descriptive name of Him as an adult was from John the Baptist. John points to Jesus, Whom he had been preaching about Who was to come and he shouts, ***"Behold the Lamb of God!"*** We don't bring sheep to church anymore, but the church is to point to ***The Lamb***.

Earlier, I asked you to look for ways the power of God might be revealed. I have also been trying to pay attention. Yesterday (as of the original writing), within a few hours I had an encounter with three people who were in need. This is not that unusual. There are people in need all around us. What made this out of the ordinary is that none of these people knew I was a preacher and as far as I know, still don't, except for one. But the Lord allowed me to share a verbal witness, a verse, or a word of encouragement with each. One was burdened because of the recent loss of both parents and was not sure how to face the holidays. Another was down because of a job search, financial situation, and having to work odd jobs to get by. A third was an elderly lady who looked as if she was simply having a hard time walking with her cane and was about to fall. After helping her to her car (I was more afraid of her driving than her walking), she told me she only had a block or two to drive home. A friend of hers had died, and she just had to go to pay her respects. After a brief conversation, she asked, "Are you a preacher?" I said, "Yes ma'am, does it show?" She said, "I thought so, you *'smell'* like one..." (Okay that was a first ... why didn't somebody tell me?). Then she laughed and said, "Old people can tell it like it is!" So much for feeling good about helping an old lady cross the street.

I would never wish on you that you would *smell* like a preacher, And we preachers are not the answer to people's problems. But we know the One Who is. Point people to Jesus and proclaim, "Behold ***The Lamb of God***!" Ask God to give you an opportunity to point someone to Jesus today. That's the power of God at work.

Celebrating Jesus this Christmas

> Where is ***The Lamb***? Write down at least one way you have seen Jesus at work in your life this week:

_____
_____
_____
_____
_____
_____

> Point to ***The Lamb***: Write down one person in need for whom you can reach out this week with a word of encouragement or an expression of help: (If you can't think of any, then write a prayer asking the Lord to reveal someone.)

_____
_____
_____
_____
_____

Pray: "***Lamb of God***, thank You for the sacrifice You have made on my behalf. Reveal to me more ways for me to proclaim to others, '*Behold **The Lamb of God**'*. In Your Name, Amen."

December 13

MESSIAH
(John 1:41)

"Eureka! I have found it!" How many times have you been relieved or excited to have found what you were looking for? Be it your lost car keys, cell phone, the place you were driving to, that perfect job, that perfect someone, or the best barbecue. This name or title for Jesus, *Messiah*, should remind us this Christmas to be excited for we have found the One we were looking for (or truthfully, He found us). But make no mistake, He is the fulfillment of what we need and have been missing before we even knew it.

When Andrew, one of Jesus' disciples, met Jesus, he went to find his brother, Simon (whom Jesus would call Peter), and said to him, *"We have found the Messiah, which means Christ"* (John 1:41). *Messiah* is a special name for Jesus. It is a Hebrew transliteration (there is that word again, which means 'sounds like') of the Hebrew name for the coming Christ. *Messiah* is the Hebrew (Old Testament language). Christ is the Greek (New Testament language). Both names mean, The Anointed One. We discussed the Name *Christ* on December 3. Some New Testament translations, such as the Holman Bible, translate the same name sometimes as Christ when it refers to a name for Jesus in a Greek setting and sometimes as *Messiah* when it refers to Jesus in a Jewish setting. If it sounds confusing don't worry about it. The two names are virtually interchangeable. However, for me, the name *Messiah* reminds me that He is the long-awaited One promised in the Old Testament. There are over 450 passages regarded by Jews as prophetic of a coming *Messiah*. Yet most of His own people missed Him. They were looking in all the wrong places. They were looking for a political Messiah to lead them in a physical victory over their oppressors. The *Messiah* had something greater in store. But not everybody missed recognizing Jesus as the *Messiah*. Some who found Jesus include Mary, Joseph,

Shepherds, the Magi, Simeon, Anna, Andrew, and ten other disciples, the one hundred and twenty in an upper room, and many more.

Don't miss *Messiah* (it's okay to call Jesus, *Messiah*) this Christmas because you are looking for (His) love in all the wrong places. *Messiah* is the fulfillment of Scripture. He is the fulfillment of all the needs you have in your life. He fulfills God's purpose for each one of us. Next time you are down, or feeling out of sorts or out of place, or feel like there must be something more. Remember those are just feelings. The reality is that no matter what you are looking for, Jesus has already found you and He wants you to find everlasting life and daily fulfillment in Him.

Call Him by Name

- Be honest and jot down some things you really want this Christmas – physical, spiritual, or otherwise:

  ___

- Does your list include something about a greater awareness of the presence of *Messiah*?

  ___

- Name some ways you could look for *Messiah* in all the wrong places or the wrong way this Christmas:

  ___

Pray: "Dear *Messiah*, may my relationship with You be a real growing relationship, not based only on good feelings or emotion, but on Your promises. Make Yourself evident this Christmas season more than ever before as I seek to find more of You in my life every day. In Your Name, Amen."

December 14

THE NAZARENE
(Matthew 2:23)

Jesus should have a special appeal to *rednecks*. Hear me out on this one. I don't want to read something into this name of Jesus that is not there. Jesus was born in Bethlehem as prophesied (Micah 5:2). He was raised and lived his life in Nazareth as prophesied (sort of). Matthew wrote, *"And He went and lived in a city called Nazareth, so that what was spoken by the prophets might be fulfilled, that He would be called **a Nazarene**"* (Matthew 2:23). But I have to tell you that the town of Nazareth is never mentioned in the Old Testament, nor is the name ***Nazarene***. However, Psalms 22 is a Messianic Psalm and states about the coming Savior: He is *"scorned by mankind and despised by the people"* (verse 6). Isaiah prophesied, *"He was despised and rejected by men"* (Isaiah 53:3). Most believe this was the prophecy fulfilled when Jesus went to live in Nazareth.

If you look up a description of Nazareth during the days of Jesus, you will find phrases like "uncultured people with a rude dialect" (Sounds like us Alabama rednecks to me). In fact, like many people in the US see the south as kind of that way, in Israel, it would be the people in the north around Galilee who would be considered more 'country' and uncultured. When Philip told Nathaniel (both would-be disciples), *"We have found Him of Whom Moses in the law and also the prophets wrote, **Jesus of Nazareth**..."* Nathaniel's response, *"Can anything good come out of Nazareth?"* (John 1:45-46). And Nathaniel was a Galilean himself. This means Nazareth must have been the ultimate capital of the rednecks with two bass pro shops, where Duck Dynasty is the number one show, and Rick and Bubba are the mayors. (I refuse to mention Honey Boo Boo... too late!)

Call Him by Name

We may have had a certain nostalgic feeling when we call Jesus, ***the Nazarene***. But when the religious leaders referred to this '***Jesus of Nazareth***', they were not just identifying Him from anyone else named Jesus, they meant it as a mockery. It was not a compliment. But from now on when you hear His name, ***The Nazarene***, would you remember Jesus loves everybody, even rednecks. And not only that, He's lived amongst us. Imagine, living among rednecks and still being perfect (and still able to love us unconditionally). What a mighty God we serve!

> Write the name of someone you know who needs to know Jesus (it does not have to be a redneck):

_____

_____

_____

_____

> Strategize one or more ways you can show unconditional love, encourage or share the good news with this person, like ***The Nazarene***:

_____

_____

_____

_____

_____

Pray: "Dear Jesus, ***The Nazarene***, thank You for coming to live in the most unsuitable of places so You could identify with anyone. Make me more like You, so I can identify with others, show Your love to all, and share the good news of the gospel with more people who need You. In Your Name, Amen."

December 15

ONLY BEGOTTEN SON, ONE AND ONLY SON
(John 3:16)

It has been said whenever Billy Graham would be asked to do a sound check over the microphone at a stadium or venue where he would be preaching a revival or crusade, he would always quote John 3:16 (KJV), *"For God so loved the world, that He sent His **Only Begotten Son**, that whosoever believeth in Him should not perish, but have everlasting life."* When asked why, Dr. Graham said, "If the message is unclear in the worship service, then at least the sound technician would have heard the gospel."

The King James uses the title, "***Only Begotten Son***". Most modern translations use "***One and Only Son***". It is a description, title, and name for Jesus from the most well-known verse in the Bible of our generation and culture. We have four gospels, each with its unique way of introducing Jesus. Luke takes more baby and early childhood pictures than any of the others including more about the birth announcements, the pregnancy, the LDR birthing room pictures, the baby dedication, and his 12-year-old visit to the temple. Matthew gives the best transition from the Old Testament to the New Testament, beginning with the genealogy from Matthew, quoting many prophecies and the birth from a Jewish perspective. Mark was the first gospel written, though it appears second. He begins immediately with John the Baptist and Jesus being baptized at age 30. John, the fourth gospel, has a Christmas story. It is short but said to be the most powerful. John's Christmas story is the verse quoted above, John 3:16.

Call Him by Name

Jesus was called the **Son of God** more than 40 times in the New Testament. At the baptism of Jesus, when Jesus came up out of the water a voice was heard, *"This is **My beloved Son**, in Whom I am well-pleased"* (Matt. 3:17). Terms like *beloved*, and *only begotten*, and *one and only*, lets us know Jesus was unique and like none other. We, who are believers, are all children of God, sons, and daughters of our Heavenly Father who have been born-again spiritually into the family of God. But we are not Jesus, nor will we ever be.

Hebrews 7:3 tells us the **Only Son of God** has no beginning or end. And maybe most important, John tells us toward the conclusion of his first letter, *"I write these things to you who believe in the name of the Son of God that you may know that you have eternal life"* (1 John 5:13). He is unique because He is eternal (without beginning or end) and He is the only way you can have eternal life (life from now on with Jesus as your Lord).

It is important we believe Jesus is God in the flesh and, yes, believe He is at the same time the Son of God. We might have a hard time understanding or explaining it because we could not be both (or either). But guess what? He can and He is both! When we get to heaven, we get to ask Jesus how He can be God and the Son of God at the same time. (Or how can God be The Father, Son, and the Holy Spirit at the same time?) His answer might be something like, "Because I am God!" (Meaning, He can do anything.) We might respond with, "Oh, why didn't I think of that?" Then He will say, "Because you're not!'

The message is simple. Jesus, the **Only Begotten Son**, left heaven to come to earth so that when we leave earth we can go to heaven. (You might want to read that last sentence again.) It is His gift this Christmas. But we have to receive His gift. This is how it is done: Believe in Jesus. Confess your sins. Ask Jesus to forgive and be your Savior and Lord.

Celebrating Jesus this Christmas

Have you done this? If so, live confidently with Jesus. Tell others you know the ***Only Begotten Son***. If you read the Christmas story in the next ten days from Luke 2 or Matthew 1, consider adding John 3:16 and explain how this is John's Christmas story. (It will only take about a minute.)

> What is one question you would ask Jesus right now if you could?

_____
_____
_____
_____
_____

> Can you think of a verse or (google one) to remind you that even if you don't know the answer right now, you can still trust the ***One and Only Son***?

_____
_____
_____
_____
_____
_____
_____

Pray: "Dear ***One and Only Son***, thank You for leaving the throne room of heaven to be born in Bethlehem. Thank You for living amongst us and taking my place on the cross of Calvary. Help me to live today in a manner worthy of also being called a child of God. In Your Name, Amen."

December 16

PRINCE OF PEACE
(Isaiah 9:6, Luke 2:13-14)

What do you envision when you think of peace? No more wars? Freedom from worry or stress? A few minutes all to yourself?

In Luke 2:13-14, there is this familiar part of the Christmas story, *"And suddenly there was with the angel a multitude of the heavenly host praising God and saying: Glory to God in the highest, And on earth **peace**, goodwill toward men!"* (NKJV) It sounded as if the angels were announcing that the Christ Child was bringing peace on earth. Is that what it sounds like to you? (Go ahead and read it again. I'll wait.)

Just so there is no misunderstanding I believe that is exactly what the angels were proclaiming. I believe Jesus came to bring peace. He has brought peace and He will bring it in every sense of the word, even the end of all wars one day at His second coming. And perhaps even more important, He can bring peace today to your life and mine as we become reconciled to Him.

For many people, Christmas does not bring the peace and joy they are looking for; instead, they face anxiety, perhaps some depression or stress. Many people are worried or sad this time of year. For some people, their uneasy feelings are short-lived. For others, it lasts for a while. For some people, anxieties come during Christmas itself, for others it is afterward. It could be due to the memory of a lost loved one or family difficulties or just that Christmas does not always live up to our expectations.

Celebrating Jesus this Christmas

It is not unnatural for even Christians to get down-hearted, to sometimes feel depressed, or to worry. In fact, it would be unnatural if we never were that way. The question is what do we do when we face some of these struggles? My Bible says Jesus, the ***Prince of Peace***, is the answer to finding peace where it is needed. And I am not so sure God does not allow us, as Christians, to go through some of our inner struggles so we might seek Him more and allow others to see the difference Jesus can make.

My niece told me this story or happening recently: A man was at the counter checking out at a retail store – he was obviously worn and frazzled and looked very stressed. He said to the cashier, "I hate Christmas! I wish that we could do away with it. They should kill the guy that ever started Christmas." The cashier leaned over a little closer and in a very deliberate voice said, "They already have!"

You and I will never obtain lasting peace by pursuing peace. It will always seem to be just beyond our grasp. But it is promised to all who pursue after the ***Prince of Peace.*** Seek after Him, "*And the **peace of God**, which surpasses all understanding, will guard your hearts and your minds in Christ Jesus"* (Philippians 4:7). If in the next few days or after Christmas, peace seems to be farther away than ever before, then be in an all-out pursuit to get closer to Jesus than ever before.

- What is the first thing you thought of when I mentioned peace?

- In case you missed it, what is the only way to obtain peace? (Hint: It is not by pursuing peace.)

- If the *Prince of Peace* were really in charge of your latest conflict, how would your attitude or actions change?

Pray: "Dear *Prince of Peace*, This Christmas, may hearts be drawn to You, the One Who can bring salvation and lasting peace. May others see in me how knowing You makes all the difference even in the midst of conflict. Help me to pursue You more and more, every day. In Your Name, Amen."

December 17

QUENCHER OF OUR THIRST, LIVING WATER
(John 4:14, Revelation 21:6)

Okay, I'll admit I took some liberties on this one. You have probably noticed by now; that these names are in alphabetical order. With only 25 days and 26 letters, I have one letter to spare, but I was afraid I might need it later and I love a challenge. (Can't wait to get to "X" and "Z".) On more than one occasion Jesus referred to Himself as the Source of ***Living Water***. In John 4, Jesus met the Samaritan woman at the well who had been married five times and was now living with a man not her husband. Even today in our so-called 'tolerant' society, she would be talked about in the neighborhood or maybe host her own reality television show, 'Housewives of Samaria'. She could play all five housewives. (As you can tell I don't know much about such shows.) Not to mention that she was a Samaritan woman and Jesus was a Jewish man.

How surprised she must have been when Jesus asked her for a drink of water. But even more surprising and intriguing was when Jesus told her, *"But whoever drinks of the water that I will give him will never be thirsty again. The water that I will give him will become in him a spring of water welling up to eternal life"* (John 4:14). Her response is what you would expect. Please give me this water so I don't have to keep dragging this heavy water jar back and forth to the well every day.

I want us to pause long enough to think about this for a moment because she is thinking about real H2O and Jesus is talking about spiritual matters. Let's be honest, have you ever read this story and thought to yourself, this poor girl is going to be disappointed when she finds out it is going to be *only a symbol*? No matter what Jesus says next, to survive she will still have to go and get the water every day at the well. I may be the only one, but I have to admit, it at least crossed my mind.

My problem is that I have used the phrase 'only a symbol' way too often. When Jesus uses a symbol or a metaphor, it always symbolizes something greater than itself. When the Bible describes heaven with streets of gold and gates of pearl, these are symbols. Don't be disappointed if there is no gold or pearls in heaven. It will be something greater. Hell is described as a never-ending fire. It might be hard for us to imagine that there could be something worse (like an absence and separation from God), but one day people might wish it was only fire.

What made the woman at the well *not* disappointed when she found out Jesus, the Source of ***Living Water,*** was not going to take her physical thirst away? It was because she had a greater need. Her life had been ravaged by sin, her sins, and the assumption is by the sins of men who had used and abused her all of her life. Jesus showed her amazing grace and He ***Quenched her Thirst*** for what she and all of us need – unconditional and unmerited love and forgiveness. Thus, Jesus could confidently tell her that He will give her water and she will never be thirsty again, because He knew when she found out what He was really talking about, she would not be disappointed. Just in case there were any doubts, John gave us this detail -- she left her water pot at the well to go and tell others. She had more important things than physical water in her life. She had met the ***Quencher of her Thirst, the Source of Living Water***.

How many times have you read your Bible or sat in Sunday School or heard a sermon and thought consciously or subconsciously, "This all sounds nice or good, but it really does not affect my everyday life, I am still going to have to drag my water pot to the well every day" (metaphorically speaking). It may be you have not discovered enough about the Source of Living Water and what He has to offer. No matter how many water pots you drag to the well, your needs will never be met apart from the ***Quencher of our Thirst***. Pray for God to give us a thirst for the things of God. *"Blessed are those who hunger and thirst for righteousness, for they will be satisfied"* (Matthew 5:6).

Celebrating Jesus this Christmas

(This is one of those times I give you permission to stop reading. This is probably enough. But I have a little more to share.) Speaking of metaphors and symbols: We have two ordinances in the Baptist Church: Baptism and the Communion. An ordinance is a church practice that symbolizes our faith. Christmas Eve, we will be partaking in the Lord's Supper at our church, also known as Communion. There are some faiths, when partaking of the Lord's Supper, claim what is called Transubstantiation. This means the bread and the cup actually become the body and the blood of Jesus, even though it appears and tastes like bread and juice or wine. Other denominations claim consubstantiation. 'Con' means *with*. They recognize it is the bread and the cup, but the essence of the body and the blood are *with* the bread and the cup. (Don't worry, I don't quite understand it either.) As Baptists, we look at the bread and the cup as 'only a symbol', mainly because we cannot easily spell transubstantiation or consubstantiation. (Spell check was a great help with this paragraph.) But let's be careful of the phrase 'only a symbol' or we will be disappointed in the words of Jesus. The symbols of **Living Water**, the bread and the cup, represent something far greater - A relationship with Jesus made possible through His Life, Death, and Resurrection.

The only way Christmas does not disappoint is if we see it for what it is – that which points to something greater than itself. In the words of that great theologian, Kris Kringle from *Miracle on 34th Street*, "Christmas is not just a day, it is a frame of mind" (from the original, not those sappy remakes). From a biblical perspective, Christmas is not just a day, it is a transformation of the heart. A transformed heart is a heart thirsty for **Living Water** and the **Quencher of Our Thirst** does not disappoint. If Jesus can *say* with confidence that we will not be disappointed, then we can *believe* with confidence. "*To the thirsty I will give water without cost from the spring of the water of life*" (Revelation 21:6, NIV). Now I'm done!... for today... (Hello, anybody still reading?)

Call Him by Name

> Look deep. Honestly write down that for which your heart truly longs:

_____
_____
_____
_____
_____
_____

> How would you describe the following as more than a symbol?

Water – _____
_____

Bread – _____
_____

Cup – _____
_____

Pray: "Dear Jesus, ***Quencher of my Thirst and Living Water***, help me to recognize during this season how You offer more than I could ever ask or imagine. May I find more satisfaction in You than anything this world has to offer. Continue to transform my heart as I drink *without cost from the spring of the water of life*. In Your Name, Amen."

December 18

THE ROCK
(1 Corinthians 10:4, Psalm 19:14)

Today, I had a hard time choosing which name to use for our devotion. There are so many to choose from like Redeemer, Resurrection and the Life, or Righteous One. But for some reason, I am drawn to Jesus as **The Rock**. The Apostle Paul tells us Jesus is **The Rock** Who sustained the Israelites in the wilderness wanderings of the Old Testament, *"For I do not want you to be unaware, brothers, that our fathers were all under the cloud, and all passed through the sea, and all were baptized into Moses in the cloud and in the sea, and all ate the same spiritual food, and all drank the same spiritual drink. For they drank from the spiritual Rock that followed them and **The Rock was Christ**"* (1 Corinthians 10:1-4). (Did you get that? Paul confirms the presence of Jesus in the Old Testament long before He was born in the flesh in Bethlehem.)

There is a Jewish legend the Rabbis taught that the same rock Moses struck in the wilderness, which provided water, followed the Israelites for the rest of their forty years in the wilderness. At first glance, it seems Paul is saying the teaching is true. But really, he denies a physical rock and says Jesus was the spiritual **Rock** that sustained them. Paul would have known about the teaching. In the verses above he is saying to his fellow Jews (and us) yes, there was a rock! But not the kind you think. Something (or Someone) bigger and better.

Call Him by Name

What do you think of when you hear of Jesus as ***The Rock***?

- Dwayne "The Rock" Johnson, the former WWE wrestler and movie star?

- Rocky Balboa? Cue the Rocky music. (Who will make more sequels? Rocky or Star Wars? I know which one will make more money.)

- Simon, whose name changed to Peter, the Rock?

A quick Bible lesson. Christ is called ***The Rock*** from the Greek word *petra*, meaning a massive rock, more like a cliff. Peter's name is petros, meaning a detached stone or boulder. It was a compliment to call Simon -'Peter', at least in regard to the kind of disciple of Jesus he would become. But Peter's name was a clear distinction from Jesus as ***The Rock***. In Matthew 16:16, Peter makes the great declaration about Jesus, *"You are the Christ, the Son of the Living God!"* Jesus responds by saying in verse 18, *"You are Peter* (petros*), and on this **Rock*** (petra*) I will build My church, and the gates of hell shall not prevail against it."* The church is built on Jesus, Who is the Christ, the Son of the Living God. The same ***Rock*** that sustained the Israelites and followed them around will be with us and sustain us, even when we wander around in the wilderness. (This concludes your Greek lesson for the day.)

My wife, Kelley, has a friend who is a missionary in the Holy Land. She began a business called, *Glad Tidings Holy Land Designs*, which employs people living in Amman, Jordan, who do handcrafts with the popular olive wood (such as Nativity scenes and Christmas ornaments), hand-woven fabrics with beautiful Damascus silk only found in the Middle East, and other such items. She employs about twenty-five full-time people in a place where unemployment is very high, such that, "doctors are taxi drivers and engineers sell lottery tickets on the corners." What makes this business so unique (beyond the Christian influence and the fact that every dollar made goes back into the business and its employees), this business almost exclusively employs deaf and physically challenged individuals who were previously isolated due to their disabilities, previously unable to contribute to their own well-being or their family's income. Never having worked before, they now earn a 'living wage' meaning they earn enough each year to provide for a family of four. ***The Rock*** has never stopped sustaining and providing.

If you are standing in Bethlehem and look to the north horizon, look just a little to the west, there is a rock, (a Petra) a cliff-like mountain which is the traditional sight of Golgotha. This is the place where Jesus walked and was placed on a sinner's cross and He provided the ultimate sacrifice. ***The Rock*** was placed on the rock so that we might have life – the real kind and the eternal kind.

So, in the next week or so, if you find yourself at the manger in Bethlehem, don't forget to look up for the cross in Jerusalem just five miles away. And then just a few miles from there is a group of special people making Christmas ornaments and such, who likely would have been forgotten or overlooked had it not been for Jesus, ***The Rock***, who offered hope. And then some 7,000 miles away in Auburn, Alabama, are a group of people and a church built on this ***Rock*** who would also be without hope were it not for Jesus. There is a difference between the Old Testament ***Rock*** and the New Testament ***Rock***. He does not follow God's people around anymore. He lives inside each one of us and like my wife's friend, we are His hands, feet, and voice for the physically challenged and to the spiritually challenged. By the way, we were all at one time among the spiritually challenged due to unrepentant sin.

Call Him by Name

> What physical attributes come to mind when you hear the name, ***The Rock***?

_____
_____
_____
_____
_____
_____
_____

> Why would you think ***The Rock*** would be an appropriate name for Jesus?

_____
_____
_____
_____
_____
_____
_____

Pray: (What I often pray before I preach or speak) *"May the words of my mouth and the meditation of my heart be pleasing to You, LORD, **my Rock** and my Redeemer"* (Psalm 19:14, NLT).

December 19

SHEPHERD
(Psalm 23, John 10, Hebrews 13:20-21)

In one of my former churches (in a galaxy far, far away), we had the tradition during most Sunday night services allowing for a testimony time for whoever would want to share. Unplanned testimony times are "like a box of chocolates..." One Sunday night an older deacon, whom I loved dearly, stood up and said, "I think we should say the Lord's Prayer more often. We don't repeat it often enough. I'd like to lead in the Lord's Prayer." He bowed his head and began, *"The Lord is my **Shepherd**, I shall not want..."* He stopped and looked up because no one said anything. He said, "I mean for us to say it together." He started again, "The Lord is my Shepherd ..." Still, everyone was silent. Now a little frustrated he said, "Come on now you all know this," and he tried it a third time, but to no avail, *"The Lord is my **Shepherd**, I shall not want..."* This time he looked up and he looked as if he did not know what to do. His wife leaned over toward him and said, "Why don't you sit down and hush up!" (If you have not yet figured out why that is funny, ask somebody to explain it to you.) It is always appropriate to declare the Lord Jesus as my ***Shepherd***!

This name of Jesus seems very appropriate one week before Christmas as we think about the news of Jesus' birth first coming to the shepherds on the hills near Bethlehem. Did you just feel a little more anxiety as we think about 'the day' being only a week away? If you are like our family, we have lots to do between now and next week. We are told, and I have said many times, do not leave Christ out of Christmas. But thinking of Jesus as our ***Shepherd***, it is not as if we are to be sure we add Jesus into whatever we are doing, but Jesus is out front and center. Instead of inviting Jesus to come along with us, we are to go along with Him. To follow Jesus as our Good ***Shepherd*** is a totally different mentality and way of thinking than most of us have had. But today is a good day to start.

You might want to read John 10, where Jesus says, *"I am the Good **Shepherd**... My sheep hear my voice... I know My sheep and they know Me.... are saved... and go in and out and find pasture... have life and have it abundantly."* Sounds like it is good to be a sheep of the Good **Shepherd**. Why would we ever leave Jesus out or not ask Him to come along with us? Let's go where He is going. 1 Peter 2:25 says, *"For you were straying like sheep, but now have returned to the **Shepherd**."* Even Jesus' sheep stray from time to time. Now is a good time to turn toward Jesus, instead of hoping He catches up with you.

In Africa, I learned that African sheep and American sheep do not look the same. African sheep and Middle Eastern sheep (where Jesus lived) look just like goats. From the front, you cannot tell goats and sheep apart (at least I couldn't). One of the only differences is that goat's tails are pointing up and sheep's tails are pointing down. The only way I could remember the difference of which was which, was to remember that goats like to show their *rear ends* and sheep do not. (The theological implications of that last statement are mind-boggling... Do I need to go ahead and say it? Here it goes...) Be sure your life reflects the **Shepherd** you are following and not something else. One day Jesus will *"separate the sheep from the goats,"* because from the front they may all look the same, but He sees all and knows all. The **Shepherd** knows His sheep.

Celebrating Jesus this Christmas

- Are you in the fold? Do you know Jesus as your Savior?

  _____
  _____
  _____

- If the answer is, "Yes" – Then do you look like one of His sheep? Name at least three attributes of Jesus, **The Shepherd**, you want to be reflected in your life:

  _____
  _____
  _____
  _____

- If the answer is, "No" or "I am not sure" – Then settle the issue today by asking Jesus to be your Savior and your **Shepherd** today. (Refer to the prayer at the end of the December 3 devotion.) If you prayed today for Jesus to save you, write down this date:

  _____
  _____
  _____

Even if He did not know it, David declared this about Jesus, *"The Lord is **my Shepherd**."* But wait ... it gets better. John quoted Jesus, *"I am the **Good Shepherd**."* But that is not all. The writer of Hebrews prayed for us in Hebrews 13:20-21, *"Now may the God of peace who brought again from the dead our Lord Jesus, the **Great Shepherd** of the sheep, by the blood of the eternal covenant, equip you with everything good that you may do His will."* He is the **Great Shepherd**! May these verses be our prayer for one another this Christmas week.

December 20

TRUTH
(John 14:6, John 18:36-38)

One of my Christmas traditions seems to be to buy stamps for Christmas cards a few days before Christmas. (If Kelley can address and sign, I figure the least I can do is buy the stamps.) Kudos to those of you who send your cards before Thanksgiving. Christmas stamps are sometimes hard to find when you wait so late. I remember a conversation I had with a lady in our church about this some years ago. She said she went to the post office the day before and they said all they had were stamps with the picture of The Madonna. She said, (and I quote), "I told them no thanks. I am tired of hearing about that 'hussy'!" I am pretty sure she misunderstood who was on the stamp (at least, I hope so). I hesitated to tell her 'The Madonna' was a name for Mary the mother of Jesus. But sometimes the truth has to be told.

Today I called the post office and they say they have just got some Christmas stamps in; some of Charlie Brown and some of the Christmas Family. I love Charlie Brown, but I actually wondered on the way to the post office who was on the Christmas family stamp. Was it a Norman Rockwell? Or Mr. and Mrs. Santa? I should not have been surprised to find out it was the true Christmas family: Mary, Joseph, and Jesus. The true Christmas family is Jesus' family. I hope you're in that family. Only those who know the **Truth** are in the family.

Jesus said, *"I am the Way, the **Truth**, and the Life, no man comes to the Father, but by Me"* (John 14:6). I will have to admit to you that of the names we have used so far, some are outright names of Jesus and some are more accurately called titles or descriptions. This name for Jesus is more than just a name, it is Who He is! Jesus is 'The Walking **Truth**'. Jesus is **Truth** personified, which means everything He does is good and right and everything He says is true. He does not just speak

Celebrating Jesus this Christmas

the truth. It is like when He spoke creation into existence. It becomes truth because He says it, which means everything else is judged by the reaction to the **Truth**. When the shepherds found Jesus in Bethlehem, they could not help but tell others. The wise men were overjoyed and gave gifts. Simeon and Anna, who were in the temple when the baby Jesus was presented, praised and worshiped. Fast forward thirty-three years and Pilate, the Roman Governor, is confronted with the **Truth** while questioning Jesus on the day He is crucified. Let's listen in on their conversation:

Jesus answered, "My kingdom is not of this world. If My kingdom were of this world, then My servants would be fighting so that I would not be handed over to the Jews; but as it is, My kingdom is not of this realm."

Therefore Pilate said to Him, "So You are a king?"

*Jesus answered, "You say correctly that I am a king. For this I have been born, and for this I have come into the world, to testify to the **Truth**. Everyone who is of the **Truth** hears My voice."*

Pilate said to Him, "What is truth?" (John 18:36-38, NASB).

Pilate was there to judge Jesus, but his blindness to the Truth which was standing before him, -- Pilate was the one being judged.

So how do you respond? One of my other traditions is to wait until the last minute to do my shopping. Yesterday, over a department store loudspeaker there was an announcement made and the salesperson finished the announcement with a 'Merry Christmas' greeting. Another employee was overheard asking, "Can we say that?" How can you help but speak the **Truth**, if you know Jesus?

Speaking the truth means talking about Jesus and living with integrity. *"Let your yes be yes and your no be no"* (Matt 5:37). I have told many a young person to keep their integrity above all else. It will define who you are for years to come. I have had questions like, "What if

Call Him by Name

telling the truth gets a friend in trouble?" First, tell your friend you do not want to lie for them and they need to come clean. If that does not work, then when asked, stand on your two little feet and say, "I know, but I am not going to tell you." Then stand back and take whatever comes. (Of course, if it brings harm to them or others, you must tell.) Better to say nothing than to lose your integrity. And never lose your integrity over something small like white lies and half-truths. If you are going to lose your integrity, wait for something really big. (But for the life of me I cannot think of anything big enough.) If Jesus is the walking **Truth**, then we must walk in **Truth**.

> The Apostle John, The Elder, wrote, *"I have no greater joy than to hear that my children are walking in the **Truth**"* (3 John 4).

> Consider what *"walking in **Truth**"* would look like for you:

_____
_____
_____
_____
_____

> For a family member:

_____
_____
_____
_____

Pray: "Dear Jesus, You are *The Way, The **Truth**, and The Life*. Today, allow me an opportunity to talk about **Truth** and open my eyes to more ways of walking in **Truth**. Also, give me opportunities to demonstrate **Truth** to others every day. In Your Name, Amen."

December 21

UNMERITED FAVOR, GRACE
(Titus 2:11)

If we pay attention when reading the Bible, we will find every book in the New Testament has a Christmas story. We know Luke's and Matthew's Christmas story. John 3:16 is the Christmas story. Even the book of Titus, *"For the **Grace** of God has appeared, bringing salvation for all people"* (Titus 2:11). Who is the **Grace** of God? It's Jesus! **Grace** is defined in many ways, but the most precise definition is **'Unmerited Favor'**. God gives us what we do not deserve – His love and forgiveness.

God's favor has always been around, even in the garden after the fall there was evidence of **Grace** when God told Satan, *"And I will put enmity between you and the woman, and between your offspring and her offspring; He will crush your head, and you will strike His heel"* (Genesis 3:15). Jesus is the offspring of woman. (Hey look! The Christmas story in Genesis.) *"But Noah found **grace** in the eyes of the Lord"* (Genesis 6:8). I am sure Noah was a great guy, but that is not why God revealed His **Grace**. Time and time again the Israelites were shown mercy and **Grace** when they did not deserve it. And when Jesus was born in Bethlehem, it was not because the world deserved it.

I have met several females by the name of *Grace*. And most, I would say, wore the name well. Jesus wears the name perfectly. He is the personification of **Grace**. If you were paying attention, you might remember yesterday I said Jesus was the personification of Truth. Couldn't I just say Jesus is the personification of every name so far, then write Merry Christmas and be done? Yes, and it would have been a lot easier and shorter.

However, there is a special relationship between **Grace** and Truth that helps us to understand Jesus. Some of you may have read

Call Him by Name

John 1:14 recently, *"And the Word became flesh and dwelt among us, and we have seen His glory, glory as of the only Son from the Father, full of **Grace** and Truth."* It is like two sides of the same coin. An understanding of both is needed. God's holiness, justice, and truth are so very important. In order for these to be understood and applied correctly, they must be tempered with God's love, grace, and mercy. Warren Wiersbe said, "Love without truth is hypocrisy. Truth without love is brutality." Most of us lean a little toward one over the other. This means we are either too rigid and can seem judgmental or we tend to overlook misgivings and just hope for the best in people. Only Jesus gets it right all the time. (Can you guess which way most Baptists lean?) If you can recognize which way you fall most of the time, it will go a long way in helping to balance and apply Truth and **Grace**. Jesus, as **Unmerited Favor** or **Grace**, reminds me not to use the word *'deserve'* very often. Let's hope the Lord does not give us what we deserve, because deserve has got nothing to do with it.

Most every year when we get together with our extended family we have a serious time when the Christmas story is read. Some family members might share something special that happened. And we will sing a Christmas carol or two. When my nephew was in preschool, which was just a few years ago, as the family began to sing, he stood up and held his ears and shook his head violently while screaming at the top of his lungs. It was as if he was in excruciating pain and being tortured. (Okay, maybe he was.) We went from serious to hilarious in about 5 seconds. I got the video to prove it (too bad I never sent it into that video show). Every year since, we sing just to watch him scream. Although, now in elementary school, he just looks around uncomfortably and wonders why everybody is watching him.

This year, when you read the Christmas story, share special memories, or sing about the birth, shouldn't there be a reaction? I am talking about more than just a warm fuzzy feeling, some kind of emotion, and certainly not screaming at the top of your lungs. But when you read about the birth of Truth and **Grace** it should lead us to respond in like manner.

Celebrating Jesus this Christmas

➤ When you sing about the birth of Jesus or read the Christmas story sometime in the next few days, what should be your response when you think about Jesus as **Unmerited Favor**?

_____
_____
_____
_____
_____
_____
_____

Pray: "To the One Who is **Unmerited Favor**. Thank You for displaying your **Unmerited Favor** on me. May Truth and **Grace** flow from my life and all of those who know You. In Your Name, Amen."

December 22

THE VINE, THE ROOT, AND THE BRANCH
(John 15:5)

Jesus is called by many agricultural names and at first it might be a little confusing. He is called **The Root** and **The Vine** and **The Branch**. But with a little reflection, each name actually helps us to understand more about Who Jesus is and what He has done for us.

In the book of Revelation Jesus is called *"The Root and the Offspring of David"* (Revelation 22:16). (I told you there are a lot of names for Jesus in the book of Revelation.) The root is the support system for the rest of the plant. Jesus is called **The Root** of David and the Offspring of David. Jesus was David's Creator and His offspring at the same time. I hope that doesn't blow your mind too much. Only He could be both. Jesus is also the support system of all who come to Him in faith.

While the root is not visible, the life of the plant depends on it. There was a coach in this state who ran a commercial soon after becoming head coach of a team that shall remain nameless. (The initials of the coach are Nick Saban.) The commercial claimed, "Champions are made when the lights are turned off when no one is watching..." In a similar fashion, faith is grown when no one is watching – in those quiet moments with our Savior. Paul prayed in Ephesians 3:17 (LB), *"May your roots go down deep into the soil of God's marvelous love."*

Jesus is **The Vine**. The branches must be directly connected to the vine or they will die. Nutrients and moisture are brought up directly from the root through the vine. In John 16 we are called the branches. For the branches to live and produce fruit, we cannot just be

Celebrating Jesus this Christmas

near the vine or in close proximity or even just be near other branches like when we gather together. We must belong to **The Vine**.

Jesus is **The Branch**. There is a prophecy in Zechariah that says, there is One Who comes Whose Name is **the Branch** (Zechariah 3:8, 6:12). He is talking about Jesus. The tree, sometimes called Jesse's tree or the tree of David, had been cut down and nothing was left but the stump. But from the stump will come **A Branch. The Branch** had a special purpose – to be born in David's hometown of Bethlehem and birth a new nation. A people of faith.

Thus, Jesus is called **The Root**, **The Vine**, and **The Branch** so that we might understand more about Him and so that we might bear fruit. To bear fruit includes: Developing in your life the fruits of the Spirit from Galatians 5:22-23, learning to live like Jesus, and bringing other people to Jesus.

Speaking of trees and branches, Kelley and I will be celebrating our thirty-eighth Christmas as husband and wife (as of this revision). We have almost always insisted on a once-live Christmas tree in the house, even when we lived in a small trailer when I was in school. Many of those trees brought new adventures. Once, it was a few days after Christmas when the girls were very young, and there were still opened gifts being kept under the tree. (More kudos to you who put all your Christmas up the day after Christmas.) I walked by the tree, and it looked as if something was moving on the branches of the tree. I looked closer and noticed a spider. No, many spiders. No, thousands upon thousands. Myriads of spiders had engulfed the tree. Talk about acrophobia (no, that is the fear of heights), Arachnophobia! I didn't even know I had it. Apparently, a momma spider, or several, decided to hatch new baby spiders, which seemed to be multiplying in our tree (I wish it had only been a squirrel). Needless to say, Christmas got put up quickly and we spent the day killing, cleaning, and vacuuming the ugly critters.

Jesus said, *"I am **The Vine**; you are the branches. If you remain in me and I in you, you will bear much fruit; apart from me you can do nothing"* (John 15:5, NIV).

Call Him by Name

Be sure you are well-connected to Him Who is **The Root, The Vine,** and **The Branch** or you will never know what might show up on your branches.

> How does the following help you to understand Who Jesus is or what He has done for you? (Feel free to glance above for some help, this one may take some thought.)

The Root – _____

_____

_____

_____

The Vine – _____

_____

_____

_____

The Branch – _____

_____

_____

_____

Pray: "Dear Heavenly **Vine, Root, and Branch,** may the fruit of the Spirit, the fruit of Christlikeness, and the fruit of new believers grow and multiply in my life. In Your Name, Amen."

December 23

THE WORD
(John 1:1)

*"In the beginning was **the Word**, and **the Word** was with God, and **the Word** was God"* (John 1:1). No one disputes John was talking about Jesus. He is the *logos* in the Greek. Meaning 'a spoken word or statement'. The term *logos* was important to ancient Greek philosophers like Aristotle, who defined the word to mean 'a reasoned discourse' or 'the argument'. John saw *logos*, **The Word**, as the perfect name for Jesus, Who is God and Who was with God at the same time. If anybody ever asks if you can explain it, say, "Sure, I can! … It is a mystery of Jesus." I can't quite get my head around it, but I believe it to be true. Jesus, the babe born in Bethlehem, is heaven's statement about God's love. God has communicated loud and clear, better than a voice from above or an angel or a prophet or the written Word (which are all very authoritative). Jesus is God and He is God's mouthpiece. He is the perfect, all-encompassing, authoritative, and last **Word**. We should take heed and listen to Him.

What is significant about November 30, 2013? If you are an Auburn fan you should know this. (I'm trying to make up for mentioning 'you know who' yesterday.) November 30, 2013 was the day of the 'kick six' or 'you got a second Bama' game. Considered the greatest play in college football history, or in all of sports by some. It won the 2014 ESPY Award for best game. But you knew all of that and more.

I spent the next year using that play as a basis for my 'one-second sermon' to share with every group who had not heard it, and some who heard it more than once. (Some illustrations are just too good to pass up.) The sermon lasted more than a second.

There are many times in the Bible when God needed only one second to accomplish His will. During Creation, God **(The Word)** spoke, and when He spoke creation into existence – it was so. When Elijah was on Mt. Carmel and built an altar and watered down a sacrifice, He prayed for God to send fire from heaven, and in one second, fire consumed the sacrifice and the altar. And then in one second, *"The Word became flesh and dwelt among us"* (John 1:14). Through the Holy Spirit, Jesus was conceived in Mary and nine months later born in Bethlehem. Jesus, **The Word,** only needed a second when the storms raged over the Sea of Galilee. He spoke and immediately the sea obeyed His voice and was calm. On the cross, Jesus said, *"It is Finished!"* And in that moment, He died and accomplished all that needed to be accomplished as the sacrifice of our sins. But that's not all. One day He is coming back and *"In a flash, in the twinkling of an eye* (less than a second), *at the last trumpet we will be changed"* (1 Corinthians 15:52), to be with Him forever. If you do not know Jesus, once you call upon Him, in one second you will go from being lost to saved, from unforgiven to forgiven, from being estranged from God to being part of God's family. That is the power of **The Word**.

Do you know what else is significant about November 30, 2013? That's the day, my family put up a for sale sign in our yard in north Alabama and moved to Auburn (although I was at the game). I officially started Parkway employment on December 1, 2013. We are glad to be in Auburn, at Parkway, and your pastor. We love you more than words can express.

Do you know what is significant about November 30, *2015*? That's the day we sold our house in north Alabama. This is the second part of my 'one second sermon' which I am sharing for the first time. For those of you who have sold a house and it took more than a few days, you know it is an anxious time. Everybody who has ever sold a house has a story to tell. Either you sold it the second you put up a sign (some of you did not even put up a 'for sale' sign), or it took what seemed like a long time. For someone who is trying to sell a house, neither of these kinds of stories makes the seller feel better because you are either wondering why your house did not sell so fast, or you are worried your house will take a long time, also.

But through much prayer, the Lord teaches lessons along the way -- we learned to trust Him more, that stuff is just stuff, and our real home is not of this world. In the scheme of things, the sale of a home is not all that significant. People are faced with much greater trials. And yes, I believe beyond a shadow of a doubt Jesus can do anything He chooses in a second or less, but sometimes He chooses to take longer for His purposes.

So, if there is something you are burdened with today – a wayward family member, a lingering illness, the grip of grief after a loss, marriage problems, financial woes, an uncertain future, the sale of a home... **The Word** can change it all in a second. There is nothing wrong with asking and believing it can happen if it is His will. But when He takes more than a second, He is still **The Word** and He is accomplishing His purposes in you and through you. After all, if you have had the one-second transformation, you're family! God always has the very best plan in store for you.

Call Him by Name

- What do you find personally significant about this name of Jesus, **The Word?**

_____

- What is one thing you hope **The Word** changes very quickly?

_____

- Will you still trust **The Word**, even if the change does not come quickly?

_____

It's okay. Pray for the one-second change and believe it to be possible, but if He doesn't answer your prayer in a one-second manner, or in the way you had hoped, pray for strength and guidance as **The Word** is working on something even better.

December 24

Xalted One, Exalted One
(Philippians 2:9-11)

> *"Therefore God has highly **exalted Him** and bestowed on Him the Name that is above every name, so that at the Name of Jesus every knee should bow, in heaven and on earth and under the earth, and every tongue confess that Jesus Christ is Lord, to the glory of God the Father" (Philippians 2:9-11).*

And you thought I was going to skip the 'X'. Those of you who are English majors have already recognized the word *exalted* in the verse above is a verb and not a noun or a proper name. What is the Name that is above every name? The verses above tell us that it is at *The Name of Jesus* that every knee shall bow. In Revelation 3:12, Jesus said to those who are victorious (all true believers), *"I will also write on them My new Name."* So there is a name we have not even heard yet that is superior to any so far.

Evangelist Billy Sunday said he has 256 biblical names for Jesus. Tomorrow I will give you my favorite name for Jesus. Maybe the Name above all Names is **Exalted One**, even though it is a verb in the verses above. It is the only time this word is used in the Bible. In English letters, the Greek transliteration (last time, I promise) is spelled *huperupsoo*. It means 'super exalted'. It sounds like a super word, doesn't it? Go ahead and pronounce the Greek word again... I actually think every Name for Jesus and all Names of Jesus are above every name and worthy of worship.

Why was Jesus exalted? When you see the word *'therefore'* in a verse, always read the previous verse or verses to know what the *'therefore'* is there for. Paul wrote this in Philippians 2:8, *"And being found in human form, He humbled Himself by becoming obedient to the point of death, even death on a cross."*

Jesus came in human form. It is the Christmas story according to Philippians. I wonder which was tougher, going from heaven to earth, or from earth to the cross? I have no doubt taking on the sins of the world was the toughest of all. Jesus humbled Himself, but afterward, He was **Exalted**. It is a biblical theme – humility before being honored. Jesus paid the ultimate price on our behalf and deserves our praise and acknowledgment. Hopefully, that is what we are doing these 25 days with these 25 names (and yet we are just scraping the surface). One day everyone will acknowledge and bow to the Name(s) of Jesus. Some in praise and adoration and others in regret and mourning.

Every so often someone will leave a Christmas present in my office at the church. If it is wrapped, I will place it under the tree and we open it Christmas morning. If Kelley gets to it before I do, she will open it quickly. I like to see it under the tree and wait. For some reason, once I place it under the tree, it is a safe zone and she will leave it until Christmas morning. One Christmas I received a wrapped gift at church, and it was in a Christmas bag (and it was kind of heavy). I safely put it under the tree before Kelley could get to it. This was 10 days to 2 weeks before Christmas and one of the first gifts under the tree. When the day came and we unwrapped the gift, I cannot tell you my disappointment to find a beautiful large fully-cooked Boston Butt, now too old to eat. (And it was covered with spiders... not really, that was a different Christmas.) Those of you who share my affinity for barbecue can feel my pain. I still like to put gifts under the tree until Christmas, but if I suspect it might be too hazardous to consume later, I will no longer put it off.

Jesus, the **Exalted One**, has been high and lifted up. He is worthy of all praise, glory, and honor. One day it will be too late for many. If you have not called on Jesus for salvation, do not wait any longer. Is it already too late? Not if you're breathing and still alive. Call on Jesus to save you today. If you know Jesus, don't put off worshiping Him, proclaiming His Name, and living for Him every day. He is worthy!

Celebrating Jesus this Christmas

› On the day you see Jesus face to face and hear His **Exalted** Name, how do you think you will respond?

_____
_____
_____
_____
_____
_____

› If your answer above is anything short of praise and adoration, stop and ask Jesus to save you right now. Sign your name and write today's date if you prayed to receive Jesus today:

_____
_____
_____
_____
_____
_____

Followers of Jesus, pray: "Dear **Exalted One**, the Name that is above every name, may You be the center of everything I do in the next couple of days and every day thereafter. May Your name be honored and exalted in everything I say and do. In Your Name, Amen."

December 25

YAHWEH, I AM
(Exodus 3:14, John 8:58)

ZION'S PRECIOUS CORNERSTONE
(1 Peter 2:6, Luke 2:7)

What was I thinking? The twenty-five days before Christmas are busy for our family and me, as I am sure they are for you. I am not sure I counted the cost of sending out twenty-five devotions with these twenty-five (or more, two today) Names. I've often wondered how bloggers have time to blog every day... and who actually reads those. If you have not been able to read all of these or have only scanned them, I certainly understand. I wrote way more than I originally intended, and never wrote ahead. I wrote it the day I sent it out, which is why you sometimes receive it later in the day. It took me that long to get to it. (Of course, if you have only scanned this, you are not reading what I just wrote.)

For me, this has been kind of a spiritual pilgrimage, like going to the Holy Land or following the footsteps of the Apostle Paul through Greece and Turkey. I am kind of tired but thankful and better for the experience. These Names have brought a renewed understanding and appreciation for the meaning of the sending of the Christ Child and the depth of His love for me. Several times this month I thought to myself, if people are not reading this or if it is not being the encouragement it has meant to be, I have been surprisingly encouraged, not by my writing, but by the depth of the meaning of His Names.

We are on a quest to know more of Him and to let Him be known by others. The more we discover about Jesus, the more we discover there is to discover. (Read that sentence again, if needed.) It does not matter if you have read all twenty-five names or this is your first day to read, we have only just begun to discover the unsearchable riches of Christ. Now for my favorite Name for Jesus...

Yahweh is considered the most sacred Name for God in the Old Testament. When Moses asked God at the burning bush Who he (Moses) would say sent him, God said His name is *'I Am That I Am'* from the word meaning 'to be', from which comes the name **Yahweh**. He is the great **I AM!** The great **I AM** came to visit us. He was born in Bethlehem and walked among us and gave His life for us. The gospel of John, more than any other gospel, emphasizes Jesus as **Yahweh God**. Seven times Jesus declares, *"I AM... The Bread of Life... The Light of the World... The Door... The Good Shepherd... The Resurrection... The Way, The Truth, and The Life... The Vine."* Each of these are spectacular names and metaphors declaring His unique relationship with the family of faith. And then in John 8, Jesus told the Pharisees, *"Before Abraham was born, I AM."* As Jews, they knew what Jesus was claiming and they picked up rocks to stone Him.

The world stands still on December 25th because Jesus is the only One with a birthday Who can make the claim. We can claim we are this or that. Superheroes (if they were real) can claim I'm Batman or I'm Superman. Only Jesus can claim **I AM** and it hold the mystery and the all-encompassing personality and reality of a God bigger than the universe Who chose to reach down to our little planet and make Himself known to you and me.

Jesus is **Zion's Precious Cornerstone**. **Zion** is one of the names for Jerusalem or the hill of Jerusalem. Jesus is called the **Cornerstone** prophesied in Isaiah 28, Who would be the foundation for a new people and a new nation. The first or chief stone gives shape to the whole building. In this case, it is a reference to the Church or the New Israel, all who place their faith in Christ. **Zion's Precious Cornerstone** is the last of our Names, but it is not the least, nor does it make our list exhaustive. Continue to search, not just His Names, but more and more about Him!

We have been in our new house in Auburn for about four months (as of the original writing), which must be about how long mail forwarding lasts. Since Thanksgiving weekend, every few days we have been getting packages and Christmas cards for the former owners. It has not happened every day, but enough to where I have alerted them several times and made arrangements for them to pick up their mail. They have apologized many times. We have assured them we are not upset we are getting their packages and mail. We are upset that they are getting *more* than we are. (More of a joke than reality, but they don't know me very well and I think they are feeling sorry for us, such that they have promised to put us on their list in the future.)

These names of Jesus, the delivery of Jesus in a stable, the outstretched arms of the Savior on the Cross, and every written Word of the Old and New Testament ... these are not intended for someone else. He is here for you! Be encouraged! Tell others!

*"Behold, I am laying in **Zion a stone, a cornerstone chosen and precious**, and whoever believes in Him will never be put to shame"* (1 Peter 2:6).

On my last birthday, the family was gathered around the table about to eat, my 3-year-old great-nephew asked to say the blessing. We all bowed our heads and held hands. With his eyes closed and head bowed, my great nephew prayed, "Happy birthday to you. Happy Birthday to you. Happy birthday Uncle Jeff. Happy birthday to you." I smiled.

A Christmas Prayer: "Happy birthday to You. Happy birthday to You. Happy birthday Jesus, **Yahweh, Zion's Precious Cornerstone**. Happy birthday to You. Thank You for Your indescribable Christmas Gift." (Yeah, He's smiling.)

Afterword

Embarking on the creation of this book has been nothing short of a spiritual pilgrimage for me, akin to treading through the sacred terrains of the Holy Land or tracing the venerable footsteps of Apostle Paul across Greece and Turkey. While the journey has left me somewhat wearied, my spirit brims with gratitude, having emerged enriched from the experience.

A few years ago, from December 1st through 25th, I crafted the twenty-five devotionals contained within these pages, dedicating each day to penning a new one. It was my intent to provide a Biblical Name for Jesus daily, offering encouragement and aiding in the celebration of Advent for the members of Parkway Baptist Church in Auburn, Alabama.

These Names have become a conduit of renewed understanding and appreciation for the significance behind the sending of the Christ child, and for comprehending the profound depth of His love for me on a personal level. There were moments during my study and writing when I pondered – if people do not read this, or if it fails to offer the encouragement intended – but, I found myself astonishingly uplifted. Not by my own words, but by the deep-seated meanings of His Names.

Our quest is one of exploration and proclamation – to delve deeper into understanding Jesus and to make Him known to others. The journey to discover more about Jesus is endless; every revelation leads us to realize how much more there is to discover. Each devotional was composed as though I were engaged in a personal discussion about each of the Names of Jesus with every member of the church. While some discussions delve into the profoundly personal, others carry a lightness designed to elicit a smile.

May each daily devotional guide you in *Celebrating Jesus This Christmas*.

Made in the USA
Columbia, SC
19 November 2023